Starting Up Your Own Home

Making Your Own Health and B
Traditional R

Dueep Jyot Singh

Home Beauty Remedies and Learning Skills Series

Mendon Cottage Books

JD-Biz Publishing

Download Free Books!

http://MendonCottageBooks.com

All Rights Reserved.

No part of this publication may be reproduced in any form or by any means, including scanning, photocopying, or otherwise without prior written permission from JD-Biz Corp Copyright © 2015

All Images Licensed by Fotolia, Pixabay, and 123RF.

Disclaimer

The information is this book is provided for informational purposes only. The information is believed to be accurate as presented based on research by the author.

The author or publisher is not responsible for the use or safety of any procedure or treatment mentioned in this book. The author or publisher is not responsible for errors or omissions that may exist.

Our books are available at

1. Amazon.com
2. Barnes and Noble
3. Itunes
4. Kobo
5. Smashwords
6. Google Play Books

Download Free Books!

http://MendonCottageBooks.com

Highly priced cosmetics may look stylish, but are they really doing you any good?

This book is going to tell you all about how you can start your own natural beauty business straight from your kitchen.

Firstly, you need to remember that it is going to take a long while for you to get going and find customers. Start small. Do not invest your whole nest egg buying lots and lots of items, because you intend to make up things and sell them.

Many of the beauty natural remedies out there have preservatives, which are chemical based. So once people get to know that you are using hundred percent organic products and that means hundred percent natural products, without a touch of any sort of chemical preservative, they will know that you are making custom-made items for them.

Let us start by the different beauty products you can make.

First of all, you need to concentrate upon what you make best. You may think that it is a lot of trouble to buy fresh ingredients or herbs and brew them up yourself and all you have to do is go to the nearest drugstore and get a proprietary remedy which you can down in an instant. So many people out there think this and that is why propriety remedies are considered by so many of us to be the best option.

So if you intend to start up your own business sense, make sure that all the items that you are making have been tried up on you, your family, and the people around you. Once you are hundred percent certain of the efficacy, you can be certain that if it works on you, it is going to work on everybody. That is because the nature has made sure that she has a perfectly natural cure for all the diseases which are present.

Ancient medicine came into existence through trial and error. Some of the recipes we read today are frankly disgusting, especially when hair oils were made up of goose fat with herbs in them. At that time, everybody was uniformly odoriferous because they were not very interested in personal hygiene and regular baths, and so some stinking – literally and figuratively – personal hair ointment would not make any difference.

If you look at the scientific basis of that goose fat, it is nothing but natural oil. It is moisturizing your hair. It is getting rid of all the dead cells on your scalp. This keeps your skull healthy and your hair looking soft, well-managed, and rich.

Also, we may find it rather horrible, but the common cockroach has been used in ancient times by the Native Americans to cure dropsy. Even in the East, these insects are caught and put alive in a quantity of boiling water – this in itself is a procedure which will have the SPCA down on me, even though they do not say anything about lobsters being put alive in boiling water, as well as other seafood – and allowed to boil. After that, the mixture is filtered. Add equal quantities of rectified wine spirits in order to make a tincture. The moment you find anybody suffering from asthma, just give him a drop at a time, three – four drops per day, and believe it or not, even the most chronic cases of asthma are going to be healed.

Many of the cures that we know come through blind chance and luck. It is a well-known fact that one of these remedies, which may have been lost or may just have been found came about; just by chance when a man walking under some pine trees found a drop of gum falling upon his hand. He just picked that gum and applied it to one of the sores, which were troubling him in the inside of his mouth. That gum cured him completely because the pain ceased immediately.

So the next time you find any sort of sores in your mouth or in the corner of your mouth, or even chapped lips, go to the nearest pine forest, and collect all the fresh resin gum you can. This is excellent as a natural healer and antiseptic.

Remember that when you are using your own beauty products and making them for others, you have to have a very open mind about the ingredients which are going to be used there. Two hundred years ago, you would not have minded making up a recipe with various muds, seeds, possibly pieces of fat, and other natural items. Two thousand years ago, you would not have hesitated at all to use skin of toad, eye of newt, and wing of bat. Do not think of them as exotic or horrible items. Just think of them as the natural source of the product you need in order to cure you. What does wing of bat have but proteins and minerals and chemicals which may cure you of some natural deficiency which is causing the disease in you.

Withania seeds

So when you are reading my book, remember to keep an open mind. I remember making up a natural remedy for one of my friends, who said her husband was worried about being impotent with the passing of time. She wanted to know all about the natural ingredients I was putting in the mixture. I told her that I was making up a mixture for her with **Withania somnifora (Ashvagandha)** and with dried ginger. She took it, and after a couple of days, she came to me and said that her husband said that the mixture stank. Of course it would, I told her. I had made it in one hundred percent pure clarified butter. How on earth did she think that guy was going to be cured?

Withania Seeds

He needed to be healed and for your interest, here is the remedy. Seriously, this is such an ancient remedy which not many people know, and is considered to be the ancient Indian equivalent to Viagra.

250 grams powdered *Nagori ashwagandha* (that is its real ancient name – you can get it from bona fide herbalists, tell them you needed for making a natural remedy and they are going to give you the right product), 250 g dried ginger (saunth).

Filter it .

Then take enough of desi ghee [clarified butter – I am going to tell you how to make clarified butter later on.] for frying it. Fry this mixture until it is dark brown.

Then add 250 g of molasses (khand) and enough water and fry until the ghee rises to the surface. 10 grams of this very powerful medicine in 125 g of cow's milk is what makes women glad to love on their husband or bull.

Incidentally, the term "bull" used proudly for a man has been in common usage down the ages in ancient civilizations. I remember reading Mika Waltari's book, *The Egyptian* in which a king is about to be executed by soldiers who have captured him. His proud queen tells him – die bravely, my bull, I am going to be with you soon – or words of that kind. And he dies bravely, gazing at the bosom of his queen, which she has bared for him, proudly. So I guess this is one word which is not going to go out of the domestic vocabulary to describe one's man.

Incidentally, if your unfaithful man has been a bit too free with his favors, – gonorrhea is also treated naturally. You can cure Gonorrhea by roasting one gram alum and 1 g Mishri (extremely pure crystallized sugar/rock candy). Powder this mixture and drink it in 125 g of water for one week. This is a known ancient time tested cure for this particular social disease.

The only problem is that once mankind knows that he can cure diseases naturally, he is not going to prevent them or mend his ways. That may make him more adventurous and promiscuous, alas.

Anyway, back we come to the natural products you can make in order to sell.

Let us start again with setting up your own small workplace.

Supplies needed

Get these items together –

1 – small glass bottles, jam jars, or any empty glass bottles because I normally do not like putting my beauty products in chemical-based plastic bottles. You can also look online for wholesale bottles, used by beauty product manufacturers. Here are some ideas.

Look for the best deal. You may want to talk directly to a wholesale seller who can get these items to you, in a timely fashion. I looked around in my city to find suppliers of these bottles, and all they had was recycled plastic. That is why I get my bottles wholesale from places like Hong Kong/Singapore/Thailand/Korea. It may take 30 days for them to reach me, depending on where I am located at the moment, and that is why I plan long-term.

I really do not like recycled plastic coming in contact with my herbs. However, glass bottles, even though they may be delicate and dainty looking have innate class and style. So set your own individual style by making a product which is unique and which is soon going to be well known.

Along with that, you will need someplace in your kitchen, some utensils in which you can cook up your brews, lotions, and potions and wooden cooking spoons and spatulas. I like the wooden spoons, over metal spoons, just because.

Design Your Label

Remember that your label is your signature. It is going to be the name within which everybody is going to know you and your product. So do not think up a long name, which makes one look at the ceiling pensively saying, that was a good product, but what the heck was its name, I really cannot remember – absurd sort of name.

My friend, who I gave the Withania remedy told me to market that product and half – laughingly, she told me to name it HotMale. No way was I going to do something which might give people laughs for a moment, but they are soon going to consider this to be rather a cheap stunt. Just imagine me introducing myself to an audience asking me what I did for a living as "you know, I am that world-famous global supplier of the Indian equivalent of Viagra, HotMale," and wait for the knowing leers from the men and scorn from the women. And then will come the bad jokes.

But nobody's going to buy the product, because hey, everybody knows about supposed potency stuff and ripoffs. eh, made of herbs and whatnot? God knows. Let us pass it. Who knows what she has put in it.

It takes a very strong heart to sell something which you know is much in demand, and comes in the personal healthcare sector – especially when it is pertaining to childbearing, ability, sterility, importance, and other such related diseases.

There is a particular market for these products, but I am not touching the subject here at all with a sterilized barge pole.

So look at your customs, traditions, and the land in which you are born. Go by traditions, but do not make yourself notorious by publicity stunts of half clad Himbos preening and strutting around red clad bimbos, just because they have been taking HotMale. And also if you are living in such conventional spots do not think up some possibly unacceptable advertising stunts like one which was popular during The Second World War, about a perfume. Here was this beautiful blonde walking down the street, just

Table of Contents

Introduction 5

   Supplies needed 13

   Design Your Label 13

Collecting Your Basic Ingredients 16

   Fuller's Earth Preparations 16

   Shampoo 17

   Beeswax 17

   Orange Peel Powder 19

   Sandalwood Powder 20

   Rosewater 21

   How to make Rose water 21

   Making Your Own Infused Oil 25

   The Slow Sun Method 27

   Quick Kitchen Method: 28

   Method two 29

   Making Salves And Liniments 31

Simple Perfumed Ointments 33

   Winter Ointment Remedies 35

   Winter Natural Chilblains Remedy 36

Natural Creams 38
    Decoction 39

Clarified Butter As Beauty Cream/Healing Base........................ 42
    Making Clarified Butter in Your Kitchen 45

    Recognizing Pure Clarified Butter 46

Conclusion 48
Author Bio... 50
Publisher.. 61

Introduction

The natural beauty health product business is a billion-dollar industry, of which the demand is growing monumentally day by day. That is because more and more people are looking towards natural and organic solutions of the ever youthful look or getting rid of skin diseases, wrinkles, pimples, or just looking squeaky clean and fresh.

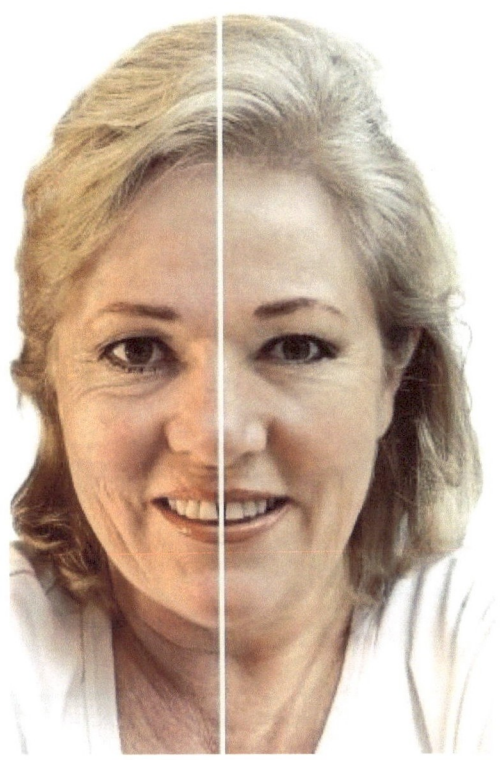

The instinctive nature of human beings to hold on to their youth, and the smooth attractive skin of that time is one of the reasons why so many people are looking for alternatives, which supposedly give them a fresh lease on looking young and looking attractive. That is the reason why you see so many brands in the market today, marketing products with supposedly exotic ingredients or secret ingredients. This is the oldest marketing stunt and wheeze, which has been practiced down the ages and it is going to continue in the year 5000.

If you stood on a market street corner in ancient Egypt, there would be some pattering show man, talking all about a magic cream, which he had learned from his Gypsy ancestors who were wise good witches. They used a secret ingredient, which were the rays of the moon, collected on a full moon's night, with a golden spoon. And as the full moon on that special night was in her full bloom of youth and beauty, so would everyone who would pay 10 obols would get the secret of the gods. Also, he would give anyone a powerful magical elixir, which would keep him looking young and attractive for as long as he wished.

Today those same showmen on the billboards talk about the same magical mysterious elixirs, lotions, and potions which have the secret ingredient of that X factor, found only by dedicated researchers in the labs and because of their truly altruistic motives and natures, they are going to give you 10 g of this precious rare cream at a bargain basement price of $149.99, when they were selling it yesterday globally at $259.99.

And you buy it. And because you think that it is so expensive it is going to do something to you, you ought to suggest yourself into thinking that you are looking much youthful and younger. Let me tell you that even if you applied ordinary olive oil and milk cream upon your face, scrubbed it, and cleansed it, your skin would feel softer, look younger, and more youthful looking. That is because you had moisturized it and got rid of the extra layer of dirt, grime, and dead cells.

wafting a scent and all the uniformed officers looking besotted – the line was Allure-Bring out the Devil Dog in Him, Bring out the Tigress in You.

Now more than half a century down the line, the word dog is quite pejorative, and in many parts of the world, it is going to be insulting.

The youngsters might find it amusing, but the older generation is going to consider you an exhibitionist and rather unrefined in the bargain, because according to them, womenfolk are not supposed to have tigress instincts, which they consider to be the prerogative of a man, down the ages! That is because in many parts of the world, even now, this sort of supposedly modernity is frowned upon, especially when it is talking freely about adult subjects.

Make sure that the design of your label has dealt with the items making up the product. If you are selling this abroad, this is necessary because many countries all over the world demand to know what products are going in the making up of natural beauty products and health products.

Remember not to clutter up your designer label with lots of information. It is better to leave some empty space on the printed paper, then to fill every inch with tiny printing, which nobody can read without doing major damage to their eyes.

Collecting Your Basic Ingredients

The items which are going to be shown to you, below are basic ingredients which you are going to use according to your own requirements and your customer's needs.

Fuller's Earth Preparations

If you are looking for natural beauty products, the first thing you need are natural ingredients, of which the first is Fuller's Earth. It is known all over the world as Multani Mitti (Mool -Taanee mitty as in Walter Mitty). – [Literally Dust of Multan]. It is the best dust, grime, and dirt remover, known to man, and for millenniums, man has been cleaning shorn wool with fuller's earth. It is normally found in chunks of stone, and soapy in feel, when you put it in the water, after you have powdered it.

Shampoo

In ancient times, women used to wash their hair with fuller's earth to get rid of the dust and grime. You can use it as a shampoo by just making a paste of Fuller's Earth with water, and coating your dusty, oily and grimy hair with it. After that, stand under a shower, and wash all the grime out of your hair. You do not need any other conditioner or expensive shampoo because you have cleaned your hair until the next washing.

Incidentally, when I was abroad and I wanted some of this Fuller's Earth, I went into a shop and asked for it. They did not understand what I was talking about. But then I talked about "you know that powder, which is used as a shampoo and also as a facemask, you call it Multani mitti," a bit hesitantly because I did not want them to look totally flummoxed and flabbergasted and they recognized it. It was not an Indian shop, but an American store. So it seems that this term is universal!

If you get it in chunks, that is all well and good. That means that you can powder the amount you want, and then when you have a really nice fine powder, you can filter it, and place it in a glass bottle.

I use a very, very old coffee grinder to do the powdering, because even if it breaks, I am not going to be breaking my heart over that broken already broken down machine. If you are crushing the stone, the traditional way, you may need a metal mortar and pestle.

Beeswax

If you are really serious about making lotions and potions, you cannot do without Beeswax.

Two types of beeswax – brown naturally unrefined and white refined.

The white one is normally known as candle wax, and is used for making candles. It has been refined to about an inch of its life. You may want to use it for making really whiter than white creams and lotions.

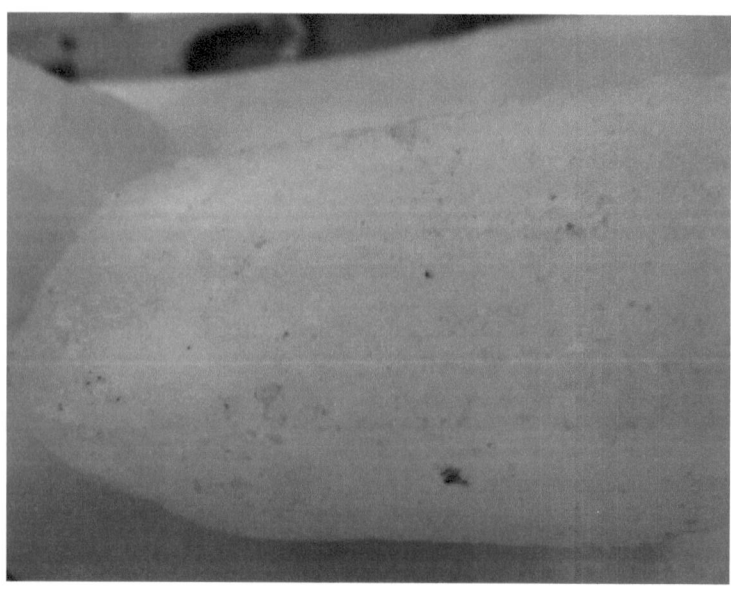

Orange Peel Powder

Orange peel powder, made up of dried orange peels – these are collected and dried in a shady place outside in the sun and then powdered – is an important ingredient, which you are going to use to utilize in the making of masks. This gets rid of the dust, dirt, and grime.

Equal quantities of orange peel powder mixed with Fuller's Earth can be used as orange peel packs. You make a paste of them with either Rosewater or cream, lemon juice, or apple cider vinegar depending on whether you want to bleach the skin or want to moisturize it. If you want to muster eyes it, you are going to need the first two items. If you want to lighten the skin a couple of tones, you are going to use the last two items which are excellent bleaching agents.

Sandalwood Powder

Sandalwood powder is rather an expensive ingredient, which however is as good as powdered almonds and orange peel for getting rid of skin blemishes.

Apple cider vinegar and sandalwood powder

I normally get my sandalwood powder wholesale for about three dollars locally. And that is considered expensive! It is going to be even more expensive when you are paying the shipping charges to your global destinations. Nevertheless, you are just going to use one teaspoonful of sandalwood powder, in the facemask powder combination you make and the 200 g box you could see above gives me about 50 – 75 teaspoonfuls, so it is worth it.

Sandalwood powder is used extensively in religious ceremonies including Wicca. That is why if you are lucky enough to get pure sandalwood powder there you are, you are going to have a sweet smelling ingredient which is going to keep your skin soft and healthy looking.

This is what I found online, get it HERE

On eBay India/Sri Lanka, the prices were anywhere between 2.5 – three dollars to more in Indian rupees. [One dollar is around 64 Rupees.] So if you can find a seller who is giving you, international shipping, you may find it a good idea to buy straight from its native lands.

Rosewater

Rosewater, or Gulab jal as is commonly known all over the world – literally Rosewater – is one of the most perfect moisturizing agents known to mankind. It is an integral part of the eastern and Middle Eastern beauty's arsenal, and that is the reason why I get it at an equivalent of 50¢ in my land, because if a woman is not making it at home, she is buying it.

So here is the way in which you are going to be making pure Rosewater right at home.

How to make Rose water

Rosewater is normally available in markets at exorbitant prices, but in many parts of the world anybody with access to the red rose – Rosa Damascena and a little bit of time enjoys making Rosewater at home. This Rosewater is used in cosmetics, as well as in cookery to impart the flavor of the Rose to your meal or to your skin.

Ingredients needed:

1 Cup Rose petals – 12 to 14 flowers.

2 cups water

Lots of ice.

A huge cooking pan – pan number one – with lid in which another pan – pan number two – can be placed comfortably.

Rosewater is just a matter of distillation. Put a wire stand in pan number one, on which you are going to stand the other pan number two. The condensed Rosewater is going to fall into pan number two.

Place the petals at the bottom of the pan number one. Now, cover the petals with water. Place pan number two on the wire stand. Now take the lid and place it upside down on pan number one, thus effectively covering the Rose petals, pan number two, and the water. The Rose water is going to condense when you place the blocks and chunks of ice on the inverted lid.

You are going to have a cupful of precious distilled Rosewater, after 25 minutes of slow steaming of the Rose petals.

Precautions – remember to have enough of water to cover the Rose petals. Also, it should not be of such a large quantity, that it displaces the wire stand.

This cooled water is now pure Rosewater, place it in a sterilized glass bottle. Use it to your heart's content. You may see a little bit of oil swimming over the surface of the water. This is Rose oil, and is even more precious. So if you used lots of petals in a larger pan, you may find even more Rose oil.

This method is for all those people who use a pressure cooker while cooking food. In fact, it is a common way to cook food in Eastern and Middle Eastern kitchens, though I was surprised to see that many of my Australian friends being surprised on being confronted with a pressure cooker for the first time. Anyway, I digress.

You would need water, petals, a pressure cooker, and a long thin pipe which does not melt, when subjected to heat.

Put the water and the petals in the pressure cooker and cover it. Now cover the thin pipe with a wet cloth in order to keep it cool. Attach this pipe on the lid of the pressure cooker where you normally attach the weight. Allow the petals to cook slowly, they seem to build up, go through the cooled pipe and collect in a utensil. I tried this way too, but I find the ice on the lid one easier!

So now that we have got our basic ingredients ready, let us start with infused oils.

I normally use red or white wine for tonic wines and spirits, and use ordinary oil for making infused oils. Napoleon Brandy/vodka for tinctures or any sort of preservation of herbs, like decoctions.

Making Your Own Infused Oil

Come into the garden, Maud, and make your own infused oils by using herbs and spices, which can be then used as a massage oil, rub, bath oil, or as a base for an ointment or cream to keep you healthy and beautiful, the easy, economical way!

I was roaming around in my garden, and looking at all those rose petals scattered upon the ground, when I remembered that I had not made this year's supply of infused oils and rose water. Now that summer is coming, ladies are going to get ready to take care of their complexions rich and glowing even in the summer heat.

And the first thing they are going to do is spend lots of money on rose water, or Rose scented lotions or rose based ointments which are going to keep them fair and lovely, so, if you happen to have the time to browse through this book, it means you have the time to make flower and herb based products!

So, come into the garden, Maud, and go to the flower bush, which has the most beautiful flowers, Jasmine or rose.

Now there are two types of making infused oils, the sun method or the working lady method! The slow sun method is for that lady, who has a beautiful garden with lots of sunlight streaming in. The working lady method is, of course, for the lady who does not have time to breathe and as she is working on a tight time schedule, wants everything done like, yesterday! (You know, my sort of Worker Bee, always looking for shortcuts done everywhere, so this can be done best on a Sunday!)

The Slow Sun Method

I normally choose a light vegetable oil like sunflower oil, but Boji used to infuse herbs in desi ghee (Clarified butter) or freshly homemade butter. I have noticed that the desi ghee infusions are more powerful, because of their concentrated power to heal.

By the way somehow, everybody in the ancient East and Orient knows that desi ghee is the best agent for painless healing of cuts and wounds.

Anyway, collect your flower petals -- red roses please- the ones which are so popular in making garlands and bouquets. Then, fill a large glass jar with a good vegetable oil, or homemade butter or ghee.

Add the rose petals until they are covered with the oil but are not tightly packed, (I found out that three -- 4 handfuls of the petals did me just fine, there was enough space for all of them to breathe.)

Cover with an air tight lid and leave in direct sunshine. The rose petals will turn brown after a couple of days. Remove them and add fresh blooms. Repeat this procedure until the oil is tinged pink. (The more changes you do, the more rose extract you are going to have in the oil in your precious bottle.)

People in many parts of the world are very lucky because they have a good supply of rose flowers as well as direct sunlight, but in the Western countries tough luck when all you sun deprived people have to go up to 20 or more changes because of the uncertain summer season and rainy weather. The more you persevere, and the more patient you are, the more this rather long method captures the fragrance of the delicate flower.

(After I show you the quick method of infusion -- the working woman method, I will give you some recipes of preparations, like ointments, liniments, and salves, using these infused herb oils.).

Quick Kitchen Method:

Essential oils from calendula – marigold are excellent for skin salves and creams

To make gulab-jal (rose water) and extract essential oils from herbs -

For this method, you need to have a large supply of petals, and lots of ice handy!

Take a large cooking pot, insert a clean brick or rock in its bottom, fill the pot with rose petals,-the more the merrier, or herbs around the brick. Cover with water and place a small glass dish on top of the brick.

Put a stainless steel bowl on top of the pot and fill with ice. Simmer about three hours depending how many petals or herbs you have, replacing the ice as needed. The bowl with the ice will condense the steam which will then drip down into the glass bowl. The water in the glass bowl is your rose water -or whatever herb extract-, and on top will be a pure layer of oil. This is the essential oil. You can separate these and use the water in cooking, or as Gulab jal and the essential oil in lotions, soaps, or whatever.

And this is the precious extract, which is sold in the market for $50 for every 10 g!

This rosewater is one of the most essential commodities of every self-respecting young Indian lady's beauty arsenal. Not only does this moisturize the skin and keep it silky and soft, but it also imparts a soft scented fragrance, which is more appealing than the heavy musky and expensive perfumes, which are alas, so often a regular and cloying substitute for neglected ablutions.

Method two

For this, you will have to have all the petals as well as a vegetable oil ready. 1 1/2 cups of vegetable oil and 250 grams of petals gave me 1 1/2 cups of infused oil.

- Place half of the rose petals and all the oil in a container with a tight lid.

- Put a container in a pan, fill the pan up with water to within 1 inch of the top of the container and simmer this slowly for 2 hours. This water bath makes sure that your precious oil is exposed to prolonged heating without spoiling the oil by burning or boiling. To save time and energy costs, I normally boil 2-3 airtight containers together.

- After two hours, allow the mixture to cool slightly and then strain it well. Now, we are just halfway through the process and the infusion has changed color. At this strength, this infusion is mild enough to use as baby oil or bath oil. Refill the canister with the remaining rose petals, cover with the strained oil and return to the water bath. Simmer gently for another two hours. Don't forget to replace the lid! Also make sure to check the water level to make sure that the water has not boiled away completely. Nobody has any use for burnt oil.

When the oil has cooked enough, pour it through a muslin cloth or very fine strainer. If you are using fresh petals, there might be some watery liquid at the bottom of the oil. Remember to separate out this liquid and throw it away, because it is quite certain to spoil the oil if it is left unattended.

Once the oil has been strained, gather all the petals in the cloth and wring them out to extract every drop of oil. This oil will keep fresh for a year but it will eventually become rancid. Many cosmetologists thus add some wheat germ oil to delay the spoiling process - (about 25 g.)

As for the spent petals, I do not throw them away, but I put them into my bathwater so as not to waste them! These oils have to be poured into clean bottles. Remember to store them away in dark and not transparent bottles in a cool and dark place away from the sunlight.

I normally make marigold, rose, and red pepper infusions at one go, thus saving lots of time, energy, and fuel.

Making Salves And Liniments

Now, that you have already infused oils, you would like to make some natural salves from them, I will help you. A salve is the oil thickened with beeswax, melted together in the ratio of 4:1.

Use the same hot water heating system to heat the beeswax and the oil together so that they do not get burnt in direct heat.

Rose and Marigold salves are excellent to make your skin smoother. Damaged and inflamed skin can also be healed by these salves. I use rose salve in the summer and Marigold in the winter or whenever I hurt myself.

In the winter, I made a red chili pepper liniment (10 tsps full of red cayenne pepper oil. Add a mixture of alcohol and water in a 1:1 ratio) for rubbing the joints in hot – arthritic conditions. Now, this milder liniment is more useful, because imagine pouring concentrated infusions of red pepper upon a delicate skin. Thanks to this liniment, the oldies of the family breeze through the winters without any joint pain.

Remember to shake the liniment bottle well before applying.

* Let me just give you another trade secret of the pain balms used for aches and pains. It is a mixture of ginger and cayenne pepper put in a liniment of Rosemary infused oil!

Simple Perfumed Ointments

The brown wax is grainier because it still has honey content in it. I got it from my aunt's honeybees. I like to use this in my own ointments, because it still has some honey content in it. So what if it is considered to be not whiter than white.

Many of us want to know how to make general-purpose ointments to stay upon the skin for a longer time. Ointments which can be used for infants, for old people, and for delicate skin. While using ointments, make sure that the skin is not hot, inflamed, or infected.

Take out your handy container and place the infused oils and beeswax cut into small pieces in the ratio of 10:1. Stand the container in the larger water pan. Carefully pour water into the larger water pan.

Here you have to be careful that the level of the water is lower than that of the level of the oil, because this oil container is not going to have a lid upon it. Bring the water turned down to a gentle boil and then turn the heat down. On this slow simmering, the beeswax is melted by stirring it carefully with a wooden spoon.

This ointment is removed and poured into clean jars before it starts to set. Do not fill it up to the brim. To make a smooth surface, wait until the whole of the ointment has solidified, melt some left over ointment in the water bath and top it up upon the solidified surface to make a smooth covering upon the brim.

This is such an easy way to make stylish perfumed ointments for the people you care, as gifts.

A couple of days ago, I prepared my month's quota of face cream ointment by melting one part of beeswax in 10 parts of Rose infused oil, in a container which was put into a bath. I was astonished when it took only 10 minutes for the beeswax to melt, after continuous stirring to make sure that it did not get burned. I put the ointment into a glass jar.

Plastic jars are a complete no-no for natural products.

Here is a shortcut method that I am going to tell you. But you will have to mix the ingredients and then thicken it to with wax. You will also have to be very careful that the herbs you use are very finely ground. I used a coffee grinder and then sifted the powder through a very fine strainer because I really do not have the patience for a hand grinder (pestle and mortar!).

Winter Ointment Remedies

I use **turmeric ointments** for chilblains in winter.

Here is ginger ointment for ooh, aah, ouch, aches,and pains.

- 2/3 cups cooking oil,

- 15 g beeswax, grated or chopped into small pieces,

- 50 g powdered herbs or 25 g. powdered spice. Here I am using freshly ground turmeric powder.

Put the oil, ginger, and beeswax into a small pan. Put the lid on and stand it into the large water pan. Bring the water to a boil, then reduce the heat and simmer for one hour. Allow to cool a little, take out the inner pan and remove the lid. Stir this all the time so that the ginger does not settle down at the bottom. Put the ointment in a bottle and use instead of any other muscle pain removing unguent! These ointments keep for many months.

Enjoy the products of your garden to stay healthy and beautiful!

- In winter, if you come to any Asian village, you will see women massaging the painful joints of old people with this massage ointment. Mustard seeds, and cloves of garlic ground together into a paste with a little bit of warm mustard oil, applied upon the painful joints, and then gently massaged.

Winter Natural Chilblains Remedy

Enjoy the winter without worrying about chilblains.

Wintertime means chilblains also, and the golden oldies suffer terribly. Last winter I saw my uncle (uncle with the honeybees from whom I purloined the wax) applying this remedy to the painful chilblains of his father-in-law, my grand-uncle who left us a couple of days ago at the age of 95.

- Heat three cloves of crushed turmeric in mustard oil until the turmeric is burnt black. Spoon the cooled oil upon the chilblains and warm them against a heater. Nobody needs to suffer chilblains anymore, ever again.

Natural Creams

Look online for creams, and you are going to see most of them with chemical additives as preservatives. For me that is a no-no. These are lighter than ointments because they have water-based extracts, instead of oil-based extracts. That means you are going to be using herbal teas and decoctions in the creams, as well as oils, waxes and fats.

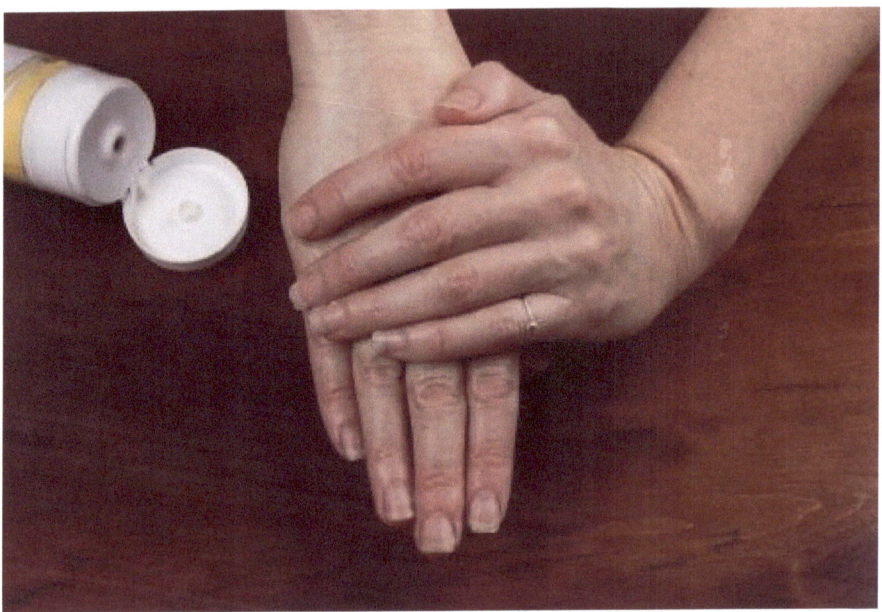

As oil and water does not mix on its own, you are going to use an emulsifying agent. These include beeswax and even egg yolks. Commercial creams are going to have lanolin which you call wool – fat.

As creams made with egg yolk, do not keep very well, without adding some preservatives, I would suggest making your creams with beeswax.

For a simple green, you are going to need 3 ½ tablespoons full of any homemade herbal infused oil. Then take 15 g or half an ounce of grated or finely cut yellow beeswax and 3 ½ tablespoons full of any herbal tea. This herbal tea is normally made up of putting some herbs in water, and allowing to boil and cool.

Decoction

Notice the wooden spoon? Decoctions are normally obtained when you are boiling barks, seeds, roots, and other tough parts of the plant.

If you are making a decoction, this is an extract of the herbs which are produced by boiling the herbs and water. This boiling process is going to be more than the ordinary boiling and cooling down which can be called an infusion.

For this you are going to crash and bruise the herbs in a pestle and mortar, and put them in a bowl and cover with the boiling water. Allow it to stand overnight. In the morning you are going to put this solution in a saucepan and add 3 ½ cups. Allow to boil and once it has boiled, allow to simmer for the next 20 minutes on a low heat.

Filter and squeeze out all the liquid and discard the herbs by putting them on your compost heap. This is now a standard decoction, which you are going to keep for 2 – 3 days and drink by pouring a cup of boiling water over 1 – 2 tablespoons full of this decoction to produce a vital invigorating drink.

But as I was talking about making creams with the decoctions, you are going to use 3 ½ tablespoons full of a decoction or a herbal tea. Or a tincture, which is just herbs preserved in wine. Put the beeswax and the infused oil into a small bowl or pan and the herbal tea into another small pan.

Put both these containers in a roasting pan. Fill the pan with water to just below the level of the liquids and allow it to boil, then turn the heat down and wait for the beeswax to melt.

Remove the roasting pan from the heat and allow it to cool a little now pick up the bowl containing the herbal tea or the decoction or tincture, carefully and pour it into the oil. Beat this with a handheld electric food mixture. It is important to pour very slowly, only a few drops at a time, and to set the food mixer at its lowest speed.

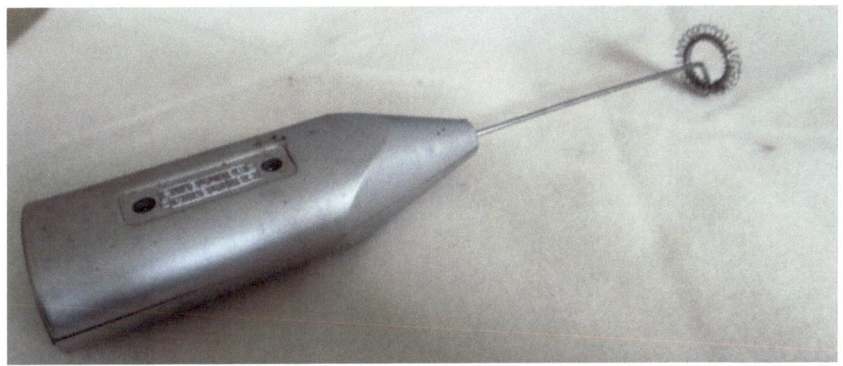

This is the latest in battery-operated handheld whippers, which is excellent for whipping something smoothly without going to the trouble of putting it in an electrically operated blender, I bought it HERE

Have some clean jars ready at hand, and pour the cream into it. When the cream is set, put the dates on the jars, and make them tight by closing the lids. These are stored in a cool place.

Beeswax creams are going to last for a few months. However creams which have been made with tinctures are going to keep longer than those made with teas and decoctions because they have all the preserving power of alcohol.

I normally use coconut oil, which is excellent as a cream base. It melts instantly the moment it comes in contact with your skin, allowing the preparations to be spread exceedingly thin and absorbed quickly.

Clarified Butter As Beauty Cream/Healing Base

This is one of the most powerful and rich concentrated healing agents ever known to man. It has long been known that people who have been brought up on a steady diet of clarified butter since childhood, and work hard so that the butter is assimilated in their bodies are going to have really strong immune system and also a long healthy life.

Also, this clarified butter –desi (as in Desi Arnaz, Lucille Ball's husband] Ghee- (GHEEE – nasal sound, G pronounced as in good) is one of the best healing agents, known to man. That is why the moment I hurt myself which is a regular activity because I am hundred percent accident-prone, I just dip a clean finger in a bowl full of Desi ghee and apply it all over the wound. I then do not bandage the wound and allow it to heal itself in the open-air. Within 2 days, the wound is completely healed with just a mild cut tissue to show, which is going to heal by closing up in its own sweet time. No infections, no pain.

And for larger wounds, this was practiced on me, during one of my jaunts in the hills when I slipped on some rocks, and gashed myself really badly. The moment I reached back home, my host immediately took a piece of cotton and wetted it in water. After that, he wrung it out. This wad of cotton was then placed in a small bowl full of clarified butter and allowed to boil. When all the water content in the cotton wad had evaporated, the ball was taken off the heat, and the cotton wad allowed to cool to lukewarm. All my wounds, 12 of them, small and big were thus bandaged with 12 little warm cotton wads drenched in heated clarified butter.

These were then bandaged. Every morning, the process was repeated and I have absolutely no infection or any scars, remaining of that particular day's activities done on a rainy day in the mountains.

When I asked my host – being a little bit of a tightwad – that he was wasting a whole bowlful of clarified butter in order to prepare a natural herbal cure for me, he just smiled and said that he kept this pure butter for ages by just boiling a betel leaf in it. After that, this was filtered and placed in a glass jar. It remained fresh for ages.

Desi Ghee is a large amount of freshly made butter put onto a slow fire and melted without burning. This is the most powerful basis of any herbal remedy in the Indian subcontinent, coming down from the ancient Aryans because of its sheer concentrated natural healing power. The longevity of the descendents of these people is supposed to be so, because one spoon of desi ghee is de rigueur, floating upon every possible surface upon every meal ingredient. But that is because they are not terrified of healthy protective fat content around their bodies.

Get rid of that headache by massaging the soles of your feet with some desi ghee before you go to sleep. This is an excellent chronic headache, time-tested, ancient cure.

Desi ghee is normally used in the making up of herbal medicines, because it is made of pure creamy milk butter. It is also used in making beauty creams, potions, lotions, and other skin ointments.

It has a powerful aroma, and that is why only just a spoonful is added to fry meats. It is going to float on the surface of the meat dish, after it has been cooked, so you need to stir the gravy before serving. Also, the food is not going to taste greasy, even though it looks like it has been swimming in fat.

Desi ghee is the concentrated form of pure butter, which is heated to reduce the butter of all the impurities as well as moisture. This concentrated butter is normally used in Eastern cuisine, for searing meat, sautéing, and frying food, because they offer its higher burning point.

Making Clarified Butter in Your Kitchen

You make this at home by taking 2 pounds of best unsalted butter and melting it in a heavy bottomed pan. Allow the butter to liquefy on low heat for about 40 minutes. Maintain this simmering point, until all of the moisture in the butter has evaporated. The impurities are going to sink to the bottom of the pan. Remember to keep stirring the butter, so that it does not burn.

https://www.youtube.com/watch?v=pfsi7rOzRf0

Pour off the clear butter and strain it through several thicknesses of muslin cloth. This butter is going to last for about a year, if it is placed in a cool and dry place. This butter is exorbitantly expensive. So in the East, people with easy access to plenty fresh milk make it right in their kitchens for crisp delicious frying results, and adding that taste of pure butter to all their dishes.

Also, what are you going to do with the impurities? Do not throw them away or discard them, because they are really delicious, when heated a little and mixed with molasses. Spread all over your toasted bread and eaten.

Clarified butter is highly concentrated. That is why it is a bit difficult to digest, when eaten on its own. However, as it is a staple for giving a nourishing diet for elderly people, it is always mixed up in their vegetables, meat, or beans so that it is easier to digest.

Recognizing Pure Clarified Butter

So how are you going to recognize pure clarified butter, especially when you go to a shop, and ask for butter oil or clarified butter or ghee? Here is the traditional way in which you can find it, if the butter has been adulterated with any other oil product or milk products.

Pick up a dried clay pot or utensil and rub some clarified butter on the surface. After a while, if you see a layer of white, where they should be absolutely no layer, which means it has been adulterated.

Take a glass bowl, and add a little bit of mustard oil to it. Now add a little bit of this clarified butter which you bought from the market to it, if there is any adulteration and the clarified butter is not hundred percent pure, it is going to float on the surface of the mustard oil. However, if it is pure, it is going to sink right to the bottom of the glass bowl.

When I told all my friends these two time-tested methods in nodded to take up the purity of clarified butter, they went around making the lives of all the shopkeepers in the vicinity miserable by asking for a test done immediately. And being quite bossy type of voluble ladies, they managed to entertain the whole market, especially when they asked for some of the well-known Agro dairy companies' clarified butter products to be tested then and there.

In fact, one poor beleaguered shopkeeper requested them to go grab hold of those particular companies' top people's throats, instead of shouting at him; he was just the innocent bystander, selling their products! This supposedly very expensive clarified butter is often made up of a mixture of different vegetable oils, to which the essence of clarified butter is mixed and then packaged and sold as one hundred percent clarified butter.

So if you want to make a healing ointment with Desi ghee, go right ahead, use marigold infused oil. Rosemary desi ghee cream is a wonderful hair conditioner. Remember it is going to smell, so just apply it in the morning, allow it to condition your hair for 2 hours, and then shampoo your hair with fuller's earth made into a paste, allowed to dry a bit on the hair and scalp and then washed off just like you would use a shampoo. And then appreciate the shine and good looks of your silky soft squeaky clean hair.

Conclusion

This book has given you some of the natural remedies and creams, as well as the ingredients which you can use to make your own beauty products and sell them locally or use them for personal use.

Incidentally, I have been using the orange peel/rosewater/fuller's earth/Sandalwood with a little bit of honey paste upon my face and nose to get rid of the sunburn and blemishes – skin patches, which normally attack men and women in their late 40s. I also added a little bit of Aloe Vera gel, – you can use cream – to moisturize the skin, especially in the winter, although I really like almond oil. Apart from this, I have used absolutely no makeup – creams, powders, lotions, potions – except of course for that necessary and de rigueur makeup statement – lipstick.

So you can see me here, well fed on homemade ghee(!) enjoying the sun, with no wrinkles, no pimples, clear and healthy skin, with just this little bit of mild sunburn, which I am going to get rid of in another 2 weeks or so. So remember that all the products that you make can be used upon yourself safely, because after all they have natural healthy ingredients in them.

This is the 1st volume of our home beauty remedies and learning skills books, which are going to tell you how to earn money on your own. By learning new skills and then marketing your products.

Marketing tips and techniques are going to be given in other books also. Remember you need to do a little bit of market research, but beauty products and health products are never going to go out of fashion ever.

So have fun making these products, Live Long and Prosper!

Author Bio

Dueep Jyot Singh is a Management and IT Professional who managed to gather Postgraduate qualifications in Management and English and Degrees in Science, French and Education while pursuing different enjoyable career options like being an hospital administrator, IT,SEO and HRD Database Manager/ trainer, movie , radio and TV scriptwriter, theatre artiste and public speaker, lecturer in French, Marketing and Advertising, ex-Editor of Hearts On Fire (now known as Solstice) Books Missouri USA, advice columnist and cartoonist, publisher and Aviation School trainer, ex-moderator on Medico.in, banker, student councilor ,travelogue writer … among other things!

One fine morning, she decided that she had enough of killing herself by Degrees and went back to her first love -- writing. It's more enjoyable! She already has 48 published academic and 14 fiction- in- different- genre books under her belt.

When she is not designing websites or making Graphic design illustrations for clients , she is browsing through old bookshops hunting for treasures, of which she has an enviable collection – including R.L. Stevenson, O.Henry, Dornford Yates, Maurice Walsh, De Maupassant, Victor Hugo, Sapper, C.N. Williamson, "Bartimeus" and the crown of her collection- Dickens "The Old Curiosity Shop," and "Martin Chuzzlewit" and so on… Just call her "Renaissance Woman" - collecting herbal remedies, acting like Universal Helping Hand/Agony Aunt, or escaping to her dear mountains for a bit of exploring, collecting herbs and plants, and trekking.

Check out some of the other JD-Biz Publishing books

[Gardening Series on Amazon](#)

Download Free Books!

http://MendonCottageBooks.com

[Health Learning Series](#)

Country Life Books

Health Learning Series

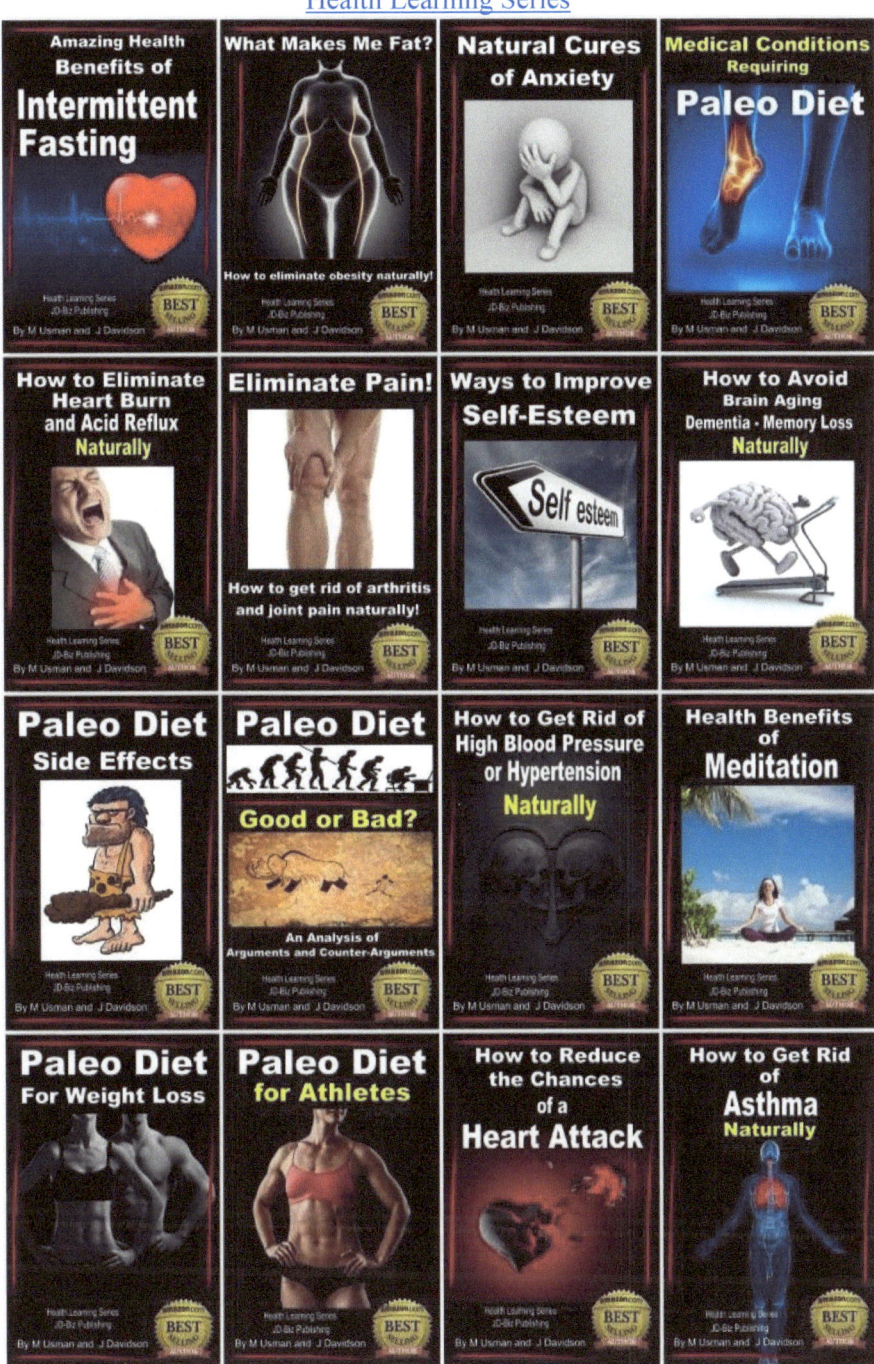

Amazing Animal Book Series

[Learn To Draw Series](#)

How to Build and Plan Books

Publisher

JD-Biz Corp

P O Box 374

Mendon, Utah 84325

http://www.jd-biz.com/

www.ingramcontent.com/pod-product-compliance
Lightning Source LLC
Chambersburg PA
CBHW042258070225
21617CB00026B/397